Following the River

A VISION FOR CORPORATE WORSHIP

BOB SORGE

OASIS HOUSE
KANSAS CITY, MISSOURI, USA

D0967318

Fourth Printing (2008)

Other books by Bob Sorge:
- *LOYALTY: The Reach of the Noble Heart*
- *UNRELENTING PRAYER*
- *ENVY: THE ENEMY WITHIN*
- *SECRETS OF THE SECRET PLACE*
- *Secrets Of The Secret Place COMPANION STUDY GUIDE*
- *GLORY: When Heaven Invades Earth*
- *DEALING WITH THE REJECTION AND PRAISE OF MAN*
- *PAIN, PERPLEXITY, AND PROMOTION: A prophetic interpretation of the book of Job*
- *THE FIRE OF GOD'S LOVE*
- *THE FIRE OF DELAYED ANSWERS*
- *IN HIS FACE: A prophetic call to renewed focus*
- *EXPLORING WORSHIP: A practical guide to praise and worship*
- *Exploring Worship WORKBOOK & DISCUSSION GUIDE*

FOLLOWING THE RIVER: A VISION FOR CORPORATE WORSHIP
Copyright © 2004 by Bob Sorge
Published by Oasis House
P.O. Box 127
Greenwood, Missouri 64034-0127

www.oasishouse.net

All Scripture quotations are from the New King James Version of the Bible. Copyright © 1979, 1980, 1982, Thomas Nelson Inc., Publisher. Used by permission.

Edited by Edie Veach.
Cover Design: Kevin Keller

Printed in the United States of America
International Standard Book Number: 978-0-9704791-6-7

Library of Congress Cataloging-in-Publication Data

Sorge, Bob.
    Following the river: a vision for corporate worship/by Bob Sorge.
      p.cm.
    ISBN 978-0-9704791-6-7
    1. Public worship. I. Title.

BV15.S6 2004
264-dc22

2003064933

This book is a rare combination of practical advice and spiritual insight on a subject we think we know but are only beginning to discover: The River of God. After three decades of a "worship revolution" in our churches, we desperately need the river of worship to flow freely in our midst and deliver us from dry and disengaged singing. This book will challenge you, whether you worship from the platform or from the pew, to step past your comfort zones and into the river.

Marco Barrientos, Psalmist, Dallas, TX

To sustain 24/7 worship, this book is a must. It is a timeless word...a clear prophetic picture of what corporate worship can become if we really give ourselves to God by the Holy Spirit. This book prophetically confronts some of our traditions but leaves us with a clear vision for the powerful destiny given to us in corporate worship.

Mike Bickle, Author and Teacher, www.fotb.com

You will be released from any fear related to flowing with the river of God's presence. Chapters 5 & 8 alone would make a great book. This is balanced reading that creates a desire for intimate worship.

Morris Chapman, Psalmist, Las Vegas, NV

God intends to use my dear friend's book to help bring about the radical changes needed in worship services that produce a most passionate desire for Christ's manifest presence. People who are totally yielded to the Holy Spirit and obedient to His promptings... Will you pay the price to apply the principles so aptly outlined in this timely book? Will you join me in interceding and promoting this "now" message from God's heart?

Joy Dawson, International Bible Teacher and Author

Bob calls all worshipers to a deeper life experience with God. His gripping honesty not only convicted me as a worship leader, but also challenged me to stay convinced that there are deeper waters to explore and more risks to be taken!

Rita Springer, Psalmist, Houston, TX

Once again, Bob calls us to a deeper place. Dissatisfied with shallow experiences that try to pass off as true spirituality, he calls us to evaluate our worship life, and plunge with courage into the depths of all that is available to us in God. Your heart will be impacted by this challenging book, and I believe the Lord will use it to continue to raise up a generation with the heart of David who are hungry for One Thing—the presence of the Lord!

Robert Stearns, Eagles Wings Ministries, New York

Bob's writings have blessed thousands and directed worship leaders to new depths of understanding and experience. Add *Following the River* to a deepening and widening experience of true worship.

Robert Webber, Former Professor,
    Northern University

Contents

CHAPTER One

A Passion For The River

And he showed me a pure river of water of life, clear as crystal, proceeding from the throne of God and of the Lamb. In the middle of its street, and on either side of the river, was the tree of life, which bore twelve fruits, each tree yielding its fruit every month. The leaves of the tree were for the healing of the nations (Rev. 22:1-2).

I remember vividly the best drink of water I ever had. The event took place within driving distance of my childhood stomping grounds on the Pacific coast of British Columbia, Canada. Driving inland some distance one fine spring day, a group from our church went on a hiking expedition up one of the towering mountains of the area. (B.C.'s coastal range has many mountains that remain snow-capped year round.)

Before long, we had left the warmth of spring behind and were driving up the unpaved logging roads into the snow. It was time to park the cars and do the rest on foot.

We encountered species of birds I'd never seen before that were so friendly they ate out of our hands. A large alpine glacier rose magnificently before us, with scrawny trees bravely pushing through the ice to catch the warmth of the springtime sun. We watched nervously as a snow system moved across the face of the mountain wall high above us, threatening the sky. This one would miss us—later in the afternoon another front would move in and force our retreat to the vehicles.

After hiking for a while in the dry mountain air, an unexpected thirst slowly began to overtake me. I hadn't packed a water bottle. But I didn't worry, for coming out of the foot of the glacier proceeded a stream that bubbled cheerfully alongside the road we had just climbed.

I stepped up to the stream right near its source, found a way to lower myself to the running waters, and took a deep draft. I was stunned at the sensation. Not only were the waters refreshingly ice cold and mountain clear, but the taste of the water was a new experience for me. I had never drunk anything like it—never before, never since. Once I had a drink, I was compelled to dip and take another. And another.

When finally I could drink no more, I found myself disappointed that I had met my capacity. The waters were so delightfully refreshing that I wished I had room for just one more swallow. After all, we've been created to thirst, and nothing slakes the thirst like water—glacial alpine water. Frigid, bubbling, pure water, with just enough mineral content to give it its own signature.

If the thought of mountain water makes us thirsty, imagine what the "water of life" will be like! One day we shall drink of an even better stream, the river of life that proceeds from the throne and the Lamb. "There *is* a river whose streams shall make glad the city of God"

(Psalm 46:4). It's a real river, and we will really drink of it. I think my first draft of that heavenly stream will be a hold-my-breath, chug-it-down-as-fast-as-I-can, come-up-for-a-quick-gasp-of-air, head-down-for-another-gulp, kind of drink.

We've been created for this heavenly river! It's our destiny! We've been fashioned in such a way that the river of God alone will satisfy the deep longings of the human spirit. David assured us God wants to satisfy these deep longings of the human spirit, saying, "You give them drink from the river of Your pleasures" (Psalm 36:8). The pleasures of God's river are our domain.

Don't Have To Wait

We will not experience the fullness of the river until we step over to the other side. However, the Scriptures make it clear that we can drink of God's river now, here, in this life, even if it's only in a measure. We don't have to wait to drink until we've passed on into the glorified state.

Jesus said this river would flow into us, through us, and out of us to others. "'He who believes in Me, as the Scripture has said, out of his heart will flow rivers of living water'" (John 7:38). This glorious river of the Spirit is available to each of us, and the greater our thirst, the greater our participation in this river (see Matthew 5:6).

We can drink of this river now! Its source is God. Daniel saw it as "a fiery stream" that issues forth from before Him (Daniel 7:10). These living, fiery waters stream directly into the heart of redeemed men and women like you and me, setting our hearts on fire with holy passions for the beautiful Son of God. As we behold the majesty and glory of His face, these living waters flow "out of" our hearts and return to God in the form of holy adoration and extravagant worship. In the process, the waters will splash over and touch many thirsty souls who long for the same river and yet don't even know it.

God has created us with an appetite that can be satisfied only by the river of God. Together with the psalmist we cry, "As the deer pants for the water brooks, so pants my soul for You, O God" (Psalm 42:1). Are you thirsty? If so, I pray this book makes you even *thirstier!*

> And the Spirit and the bride say, "Come!"
> And let him who hears say, "Come!" And let
> him who thirsts come. Whoever desires, let
> him take the water of life freely (Revelation
> 22:17).

May we be so desperate for this river that we become willing to do whatever it takes to find it, stay in it, and point the way for others.

This is a book about worship—specifically, corporate worship. There is a river to be found in worship that satisfies the thirsty soul. I have looked seriously at the question, "Where is God taking us in our worship?" No one would question that we have experienced a revival in worship in recent years. And yet, where is it all going? This book is a beginning attempt to answer that question. Each chapter will reveal another layer of the vision. By the time we're finished, I pray you will carry a blazing passion for the powerful potential in corporate worship.

CHAPTER TWO

Swimming-Depth Waters

Ezekiel was shown the river of God in what is perhaps the most graphic description of this river in the entire Bible. As we look at Ezekiel's river, I would like us to view it as depicting *the river of corporate worship*. This is not the only way to interpret this passage, but it certainly is one of the valid interpretations.

There is a river that flows in corporate worship. It derives from the very throne of God, and quenches the thirst of God's people. Ezekiel's vision of this river was truly visionary in that it wasn't a fanciful imagination of what *could* be but was a revelation of what most certainly *will* be. This river is coming, and I'm contending for it in my generation. Come with me as we look at this river of corporate worship.

> Then he brought me back to the door of the temple; and there was water, flowing from under the threshold of the temple toward the east, for the front of the temple faced east; the water was flowing from under the right side of the temple, south of the altar.

> He brought me out by way of the north gate,
> and led me around on the outside to the
> outer gateway that faces east; and there
> was water, running out on the right side
> (Ezekiel 47:1-2).

This water, running out of the right side of the temple,
reminds us of the water that flowed from the side of Christ
when He was pierced by the soldier (John 19:34). That
wound in Christ's side opened the channel for a river of life
to flow forth from Christ's broken heart to a desperately
thirsty world. The river of God finds its origination in the
crucified Lamb. That's why, when we focus upon the Lamb,
we often find ourselves flowing in the deepest waters of
worship. Nothing unlocks the affections of a lovesick Bride
more than when she beholds, by faith, her Beloved impaled
upon His cross. Here is where the river flows.

Going Deeper

> And when the man went out to the east
> with the line in his hand, he measured one
> thousand cubits, and he brought me through
> the waters; the water came up to my ankles.
> Again he measured one thousand and
> brought me through the waters; the water
> came up to my knees. Again he measured
> one thousand and brought me through;
> the water came up to my waist. Again he
> measured one thousand, and it was a river
> that I could not cross; for the water was too
> deep, water in which one must swim, a river
> that could not be crossed (Ezekiel 47:3-5).

Ezekiel is led down the river in increments of roughly
one third of a mile (one thousand cubits) at a time, and

the waters go from his ankles to his knees, to his waist, to "water in which one must swim." It is striking that the river grows in volume with no other tributaries feeding it. There is something about the river that is self-generating, causing the river to grow from a trickle to a flood in little more than a mile. Ezekiel is being shown how we can progress from the shallows of the river to its greatest depths, a progression that can be experienced powerfully in corporate worship.

There is a flow to be found in corporate worship that is so deep and compelling that the waters cannot be crossed. I am weary of watching seekers and sinners pass through the river of our worship services and come up the other side, for the most part, untouched. They leave a little bit damp, saying, "They have good music in that church." Or they may say, "Nice service." My heart aches every time I hear such plastic compliments from inquirers because I realize they've experienced far less among God's people than what Jesus died to provide.

I will tell you what I'm looking for. My heart cries out, "God, give us such a depth in the river of God in worship that people are swept off their feet in the glory of this lifegiving flow! Give us worship services that can't be crossed!" I'm looking for those times when it doesn't matter in what condition you entered the worship service—whether an agnostic, a seeker, an atheist, an antagonist, a skeptic, a hypocrite, a believer, an unbeliever, a saint, a sinner, a Holy Ghost-filled on-fire fanatic, or a bored, stiff-necked, hard-hearted cynic. When the river of worship finds this kind of depth in God, *nobody* is able to remain unchanged! It sweeps everyone in the room off their feet.

I can't think of anything more fitting for today's generation than a sweep-you-off-your-feet encounter with God in the river of His delights. An encounter with God

Almighty will place a mark upon youth for life that will
never be forgotten. When the winds of temptation or peer
pressure swirl around their lives, they will never be able
to forget those times when God visited them in power and
glory.

The Trees Of Healing

He said to me, "Son of man, have you seen
this?" Then he brought me and returned me
to the bank of the river. When I returned,
there, along the bank of the river, were very
many trees on one side and the other. Then
he said to me: "This water flows toward the
eastern region, goes down into the valley,
and enters the sea. When it reaches the sea,
its waters are healed. And it shall be that
every living thing that moves, wherever
the rivers go, will live. There will be a
very great multitude of fish, because these
waters go there; for they will be healed, and
everything will live wherever the river goes"
(Ezekiel 47:6-9).

Ezekiel didn't see the trees of healing until he got to
swimming-depth in the river. When we encounter this
depth worship, we will touch the dimension of glory where
healings and miracles will return to the house of prayer,
exactly where they belong (Matthew 21:14).

When this passage speaks of "the sea," it's a reference
to what we call the Dead Sea or Salt Sea. The Dead Sea
is a lake in Palestine that is fed by the Jordan River and
has no outlet, but loses its moisture via evaporation alone.
Since it has no outlet, its waters are extremely salty,
much more so even than the ocean, and therefore it does
not support any aquatic life whatsoever. It's a dead sea.
This is why Ezekiel's description is so significant. These

waters bring healing to places that have been haunts of death. This river heals that which is caustic and turns a place of death into a place of teeming life.

Many of today's denominations and fellowship groups have churches sprinkled throughout their ranks that are like the Dead Sea. Where there had been life, there is now death. Ezekiel is making a prophetic declaration over those pockets in the church that have grown cold and dead and salty. He is saying, "You are not beyond recovery. There is something that will renew your spiritual vitality as a church, as a movement. It is the river of God that is released and realized in corporate worship!" We are watching Ezekiel's prophecy being fulfilled before our eyes. There is a wave of renewal hitting many churches that seemed to be beyond hope, and the new life they are finding is specifically because of corporate worship. They are finding the river in worship, and it's breathing new life into dead formalism. It's awesome to behold! And it's only going to increase.

Here's the conclusion of Ezekiel's vision.

> "It shall be that fishermen will stand by it from En Gedi to En Eglaim; they will be places for spreading their nets. Their fish will be of the same kinds as the fish of the Great Sea, exceedingly many. But its swamps and marshes will not be healed; they will be given over to salt. Along the bank of the river, on this side and that, will grow all kinds of trees used for food; their leaves will not wither, and their fruit will not fail. They will bear fruit every month, because their water flows from the sanctuary. Their fruit will be for food, and their leaves for medicine" (Ezekiel 47:10-12).

Again, we see many fish drawn to these waters, and we see a constant release of healing powers released through this river. Somebody might ask, "But if we really get into the depths of the river of God in our corporate worship services, won't we scare away the very fish we're trying to catch?" The way Ezekiel saw it unfolding, the fish were attracted to the healing and life that flowed in this river.

If you really get into the flow of God's river in corporate worship, you might scare some of the beasts away; but the true fish whom the Master is drawing will find the river the very thing for which they have been yearning.

CHAPTER Three

River-Hunting

The greatest delights of the river are to be found, not at the banks, but in the middle of the river. My friend, Gary Wiens, tells about the time some friends took him white-water rafting in the mountains of Colorado. He says it was thrilling to traverse stage-four rapids and come through in one piece. They encountered one series of stage-five rapids (the most turbulent stage on the intensity scale), and Gary told me it was an unparalleled rush to be so totally out of control. He said, "The only thing that makes it work is the presence of a good guide."

We need not fear the swift currents of God's glorious river. Beloved saints, we have a good Guide. The Holy Spirit is our very capable Guide in this holy river of corporate worship, and while there are potential dangers in the more turbulent waters, there are also unparalleled thrills. The river is our destiny! But it's not automatic, we must seek this river with all our hearts.

Paul's Perspective

Paul had a contagious pespective on the powerful potential of corporate worship. When he articulated it, he did not use the river imagery of Ezekiel 47, but yet he spoke of the same spiritual momentum that can be experienced when God's people gather in worship. Paul had his own way of describing what happens. He wrote:

> But if all prophesy, and an unbeliever or an uninformed person comes in, he is convinced by all, he is convicted by all. And thus the secrets of his heart are revealed; and so, falling down on his face, he will worship God and report that God is truly among you (1 Corinthians 14:24-25).

When God's people begin to truly worship in Spirit and in truth, something begins to take over the meeting. Ezekiel called it a river. Paul referred to it as a prophetic anointing ("if all prophesy"), which has the power to sweep an entire congregation into the river of spiritual worship. When a prophetic anointing explodes in a corporate worship context, there are four things that can potentially take place.

The first thing that happens, according to Paul, is the secrets of the uninformed are revealed. The Holy Spirit knows them implicitly, and He is able through His gifts to give prophetic messages to others in the congregation that speak directly to their lives (see 1 Corinthians 14). The Holy Spirit does not use these gifts to embarrass people by revealing shameful details about their lives. That's not what Paul is talking about. Rather, the Holy Spirit will inspire a message through a human vessel that will stun the unbeliever with the realization that God knows him.

God sees him. God understands the deep longings of his soul. God is interested in him.

Next, the verse says the unbeliever will fall on his face. I can imagine this happening through the convicting power of the Holy Spirit. When the uninformed person realizes how intimately he is known and understood by God, he will fall on his face in the presence of God's holiness. When was the last time you had an unbeliever fall on his face in one of your worship services? According to Paul, it should not be an uncommon occurrence.

Third, it says "he will worship God." It doesn't say necessarily that he is converted or born again, because he doesn't have to be a believer in Jesus to worship God. Even the ungodly can give glory to God. God is able to bring even the rebels to their knees in worship, acknowledging His power, wisdom, and majesty.

And finally, he will "report that God is truly among you." He'll go away from the meeting saying to his friends, "If you go to that church, you will meet up with God. I'm serious—God is in that place!" He may be so terrified that he'll swear to himself, "That's the last time I'm ever stepping inside the doors of that church!" And then...next week...he's probably back again! Why? Because once you've tasted of the goodness of God, you're ruined for anything less.

Thank you, Paul, for giving us such a glorious picture of where worship can take us! It makes us long to find this great river in God.

You will notice that Paul's criteria for a successful worship service was not based upon what the believers thought when they left the meeting. The New Testament litmus test for corporate worship is: *what did the unbelievers say about the meeting after they left?* Did they come away testifying to the immediacy of God in the meeting?

Take Soundings

Once you've experienced this river of divine pleasures in corporate worship, you begin to develop the ability to discern when a worship gathering has found the river. You'll find yourself thinking, "Not yet. We're not there yet. We're getting close, but we haven't hit the river yet in this meeting." And then sometimes you'll find yourself thinking, "Ah, now we're getting somewhere. Now I can sense that things are starting to move in the Spirit realm. I believe we've just hit water. This is the beginning of the river."

In congregational worship, worship leaders are constantly reaching out in their spirits to discern when the meeting touches the river of God. They'll throw out a song—and then search with their toes (in a metaphorical sense) to see if their feet have found water.

"Nope. No water yet. Let's try the next song."

So they'll throw out the next song on their list. As they're singing through the song, they're still searching for the kind of divine flow that will take over the worship service. It's called river-hunting.

"Still nothing. Whew. Let's hope the next song produces something."

And so worship leaders will tend to go through their songlist, one song after another, hoping that at some point in the worship service we will somehow find the river of God. They strain to find the thing God's Spirit is wanting to breathe upon as we have gathered in Christ's name. When the river of God catches up a worship service, we find ourselves carried along by a divine impetus. God Himself is energizing our worship. Trying to sustain a worship service with musical means and human strength is one of the most wearisome chores a leader will ever attempt.

But oh, when God takes the meeting! When that happens, leading worship is one of the most exhilarating joys God can give to His leaders.

It's critical for worship leaders to develop their discernment as regards the river of God. There are three things to be watching for. They need to know when a worship service has hit the river, they need to know when we're moving forward into deeper waters, and they also need to learn to recognize when we're moving away from the river.

When a worship time doesn't find the kind of flow the worship leaders desire, it's tempting for the leaders to become introspective and try to figure out what they're doing wrong. Keep this in mind: *Our job as worship leaders is to do our best to find the river and stay in it—God determines the depth.* Sometimes He leads us into awesome depths, and at other times He keeps us in the shallows. The depth of the river is sovereignly controlled by the hand of God. After searching for the river, we must be content with the depth God chooses to give in the moment.

I've been in many worship services in which we've hit the river of God, but the worship leaders didn't know how to keep us in the river. The entire congregation was aware that we had just hit water, and a wave of anticipation rippled through the crowd. But then we began to move into the shallows, and it's as though the leaders don't know how to change direction. So we just kept moving into shallower water until we were back on land again.

Sometimes I've wanted to wave a warning flag from my place in the congregation: "Danger! If we keep this course, we're going to leave the thing that God is breathing upon in this meeting. Let's go back to where the current was stronger."

Worship leaders must develop the ability to take

soundings. I have Acts 27:28-29 in view, "And they took soundings and found it to be twenty fathoms; and when they had gone a little farther, they took soundings again and found it to be fifteen fathoms. Then, fearing lest we should run aground on the rocks, they dropped four anchors from the stern, and prayed for day to come."

Those who have experience navigating waters are well aware that when you take a sounding (to measure how deep the water is), and the depth of water is decreasing rapidly, you are running the risk of hitting land.

As we navigate our way in the river of God, it's essential for worship leaders to not only learn how to *find* the river of God, but also learn how to *stay* in the river of God. It requires flexibility to change direction when we perceive that our current direction is taking us away from the deeper waters of the Spirit's flow in worship.

CHAPTER Four

The River Versus The Songlist

One day, as I was meditating upon the river of God, I was suddenly struck with this very simple realization: *Rivers don't follow straight lines.*

Service orders do, however. Service orders are drafted in a straight line of item one, item two, item three, etc.

Songlists follow straight lines, too. Songlists are a vertical listing of songs, one after the other. Boom, boom, boom, down the list we go.

The river of God, in contrast, does not follow straight lines. It follows an unpredictable path of turns and changes. You could be in a time of intimacy when suddenly a spirit of celebration will erupt. Or you may be exalting the majesty of God when the river will take a sudden turn and spur you into an expression of spiritual warfare. Those who have not learned to respond to the Spirit's fluid movements will be deprived of the thrill of moving with God, at least to the degree their souls desire.

River Diagrams

The following diagrams depict various types of worship services. The curved line represents the river of God—the river that we long to find in corporate worship. This river is the place where healings happen, where a prophetic spirit fills the auditorium, and where sinners begin to fall on their faces under the convicting power of the Holy Spirit as He is revealing the deep cry of their hearts. Oh, how we long for this river!

The straight line in each diagram, with the arrow at the end, is representative of our songlist (since songlists move in straight lines). We are using these diagrams to show the relationship between the flowing river of God and the straight lines of our service preparation.

Fig. 1, The landlubber service

In the worship service represented by this diagram, you'll notice that the songlist is moving completely parallel to the river of God. In other words, as long as we stay with the songlist, we will never encounter the river.

This is the most depressing worship service anyone can possibly endure. In this service, the worship leaders are trying to find the river of God, and they're hoping with every successive song that something will change. But no matter what song they pull out from their list, there is no water to be found. But they're so desirous of finding the river that they just keep on moving through their list, hoping that eventually one of the songs will cause a change in the meeting.

I don't fully understand why God allows us to have these kinds of frustrating services at times. Maybe He is reminding us that the Kingdom of God will never move forward in human strength and planning. "Not by songlist, nor by service order, but by My Spirit, says the Lord of hosts." Maybe He is wanting us to have a lousy service simply for the sake of contrast, so that when we find the river we'll really be appreciative. Or maybe there is a spiritual hindrance that needs to be discerned and overcome. Or maybe He's disciplining us, wanting us to become dislodged from our comfort zones. After all, it feels very safe to remain within the borders of our list of songs that we've practiced. But maybe He wants us to get out of the boat of our preparation and start walking on the waters of songs and expressions we hadn't planned.

Whatever God's reasons in each particular case, the fact remains that some worship services are dry from start to finish. To be honest, I've endured my share of these types of services. I feel like I've filled up my lifetime quota already. So if I never see another worship service like this one for the rest of my life, I wouldn't miss it for a moment.

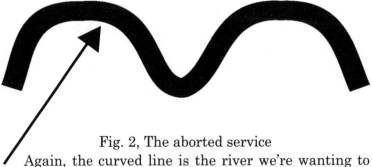

Fig. 2, The aborted service
Again, the curved line is the river we're wanting to

find, and the straight line represents our linear songlist. In this service, our songlist is actually taking us in the right direction. If we stay on course, we'll eventually hit water.

You'll notice, however, that the worship service doesn't quite make it to the river. That's because, just as we're about to hit water we hear those famous words, *"You may be seated."*

Fig. 3, The quit-while-you're-ahead service

In this worship service, we're moving through our list of songs, looking earnestly for the river. Then something begins to happen. We sense a breeze of the Spirit moving through the room. Expectant hearts begin to turn heavenward. The presence of Jesus begins to gently distill in the room in a way that everyone can sense. There's no mistaking it; we have encountered the presence of the living Christ. Waters are beginning to swirl gently around our feet. We've found the river of God!

This is what we came together for! We have gathered together in His name because we wanted to touch the life-changing river of God, and now it is happening. How thankful we are to God for this moment.

Then—very smoothly, so as not to appear disruptive—one of the leaders glides over to a microphone and saves the service from potential trouble. There is the fear that an unstable saint, moved by the freshness of the waters, could erupt in an expression of exuberance that might be misunderstood by others. But the even greater fear is: Now that we've touched the river, if we keep moving with the worship service, we might lose something that we've just now found, and end up with something anticlimactic. So, to avoid any kind of let-down, we quickly and gently bring the worship service to an end, and move on to the next portion of the service order.

This wisdom says, "Once you find the river, quit while you're ahead."

But I can't help but respond, "Once we find the river, why can't we enjoy it for a while? Now that we're up to our ankles, why can't we venture forward into deeper waters, up to our knees, or our waists, or perhaps even waters to swim in?" We haven't come this far to take a quick sip and sit down. We've come this far so we could drink deeply of the river that "makes glad the city of God."

Fig. 4, The tunnel vision service

In this worship service, we're moving through our songlist when suddenly it happens! We hit the river! Faces are turned upwards, tears begin to flow, hearts begin to soar on the winds of the Spirit.

But the worship leaders just keep moving with their

list. For a while everyone still thinks we're in the river because everybody is wet. But guess what? You're no longer in the river, you're back on land.

When we hit the river in worship, the river can actually appear to be a detour. The river is flowing one way, and our songlist is going another way. Worship leaders are sometimes faced with a very awkward decision. Sometimes they have to choose between the river and the next song on the list.

Going with the songlist is like staying in the boat; it's safe, predictable, and dry. Going with the river is like walking on water; it's unpredictable, potentially hazardous, and filled with uncertainty. And following the river can be very disruptive to service orders. Sometimes we pay a price to follow the river. Leaders often have to make split-second decisions to either go with the river or go with their list.

Those who have walked with Jesus long enough have learned that it's safer to be out on the water with Jesus than to be in the boat without Him. But walking on water *looks* more dangerous.

Sometimes worship leaders look in two directions. They look, first, at the river of God, and to what God is inviting them. Then they look out at the people. And they're asking themselves this question, "Is this group of saints ready to get out of the boat and walk with us on water?" To put it another way, "Are these people ready to flow with us, and enter together with us into the river of God right now?"

Sometimes the leaders look out at the congregation and see half of them disengaged, some of them staring into space, others looking downright miserable, while others are checking out the room or whispering to their neighbor. And the leaders say to themselves. "Naw. Not this group. Not today." And instead of stepping out courageously into the unknown territory of flowing with the river, they revert to the safety net of their songlist and just plod ahead with their preparation.

If worshipers want their leaders to have the fortitude to go with the river, they need to be reflecting encouragement back to the leaders with their postures and expressions, indicating through their participation that they are ready to go with the flow. When worshipers are engaged and proactive, they are sending signals to the worship leaders, "Go for it! We're ready! Be courageous! Be strong! Launch into the deep. You're not on your own, we're with you. Let's see where God might take us today."

Fig. 5, The U-turn service

Like the worship service in Diagram 3, we're moving forward with our list, we hit the river of God, but then we keep on moving straight ahead with our songlist. However, a few minutes later we stop and say to ourselves, "Hey, there's water back there!" So then the worship leaders take a hard turn and head back to find the river again.

When you're not hitting water in a worship service, but you want to, it seems to me that worship leaders have two general options at their disposal. Option one is to persevere, to keep knocking at the door, to keep pressing forward on the present course and hope for a breakthrough to eventually come. Option two is to stop, change course, and pursue the river in a different direction or a different way. (For example, there are times when you will not find the river through the singing of songs. Sometimes the key to the worship service will be found through a non-musical expression, such as an altar call, or repentance, or taking the Lord's Supper, or waiting in quietness, or through the sermon, etc.) Only the Spirit of God knows which of these two responses is right for the moment at hand. We are so dependent upon His guidance.

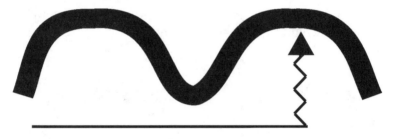

Fig. 6, The standard charismatic service

This diagram represents the liturgy of many contemporary churches today. It seems someone must have written a rule, "You can't go river-hunting until you're 25 minutes into a worship service. For the first 25 minutes, don't even expect to encounter water. Do your songlist. Then, after you've sung three fast songs and three slow songs, you can begin to search for the river."

I am raising a formal objection to this prevailing custom of our day. My heart cries out, "Why can't we go river-hunting right from the start of the meeting?" Whoever wrote the rule that you have to wait for 25 minutes before you can get out of the boat—let's form a posse and hang the guy.

Let's start a new liturgy. Let's make it our custom

to go hunting for the river of God immediately from the outset of our worship services. Why use up our time on preliminaries when we can pursue the heart of God from the start of the very first song?

Fig. 7, The so-close-you-can-taste-it service

In this service, we're in the river; then we're out of the river; then we're back in; then we're back on land; then we're back in the water again. Our songlist seems to follow the river so closely that we're moving in and out as the service progresses.

Here's what I'm suggesting in this chapter: There is a *fundamental incompatibility* between the straight lines of our preparation and the flow of the Spirit. It is impossible to remain within the straight lines of our preparation and expect to flow in the depths of the river of God's glory. Inevitably, we must choose between the comfortable safety of our songlist and the veiled uncertainty of following the river of God. Rarely can we have both.

If I could presume to speak for all the lovesick worshipers of the earth, I would like to say to all the worship leaders of the earth, "We don't want your songlist; we want the river!"

CHAPTER Five

The Tension Between Preparation and Spontaneity

irst off, I want to clarify some things from the last chapter. Someone could misunderstand me to be naysaying preparation. For the record, I am *pro-preparation*. I am a strong advocate for the need of a worship ministry to practice, to rehearse, and to prepare for the corporate worship context. *Preparation is essential.* The Sunday morning worship service should not be used to practice on the people!

The Scriptures exhort us, "Having shod your feet with the preparation of the gospel of peace" (Ephesians 6:15). We are told to have our feet shod with shoes. But what exactly are these shoes? Are they the shoes of *peace*? No, they are the shoes of *preparation*. When you are properly prepared, it's like going to war with your shoes on. You would never want to enter the battle barefoot! Being properly prepared for worship is like getting shod for battle.

So I strongly support the need for preparation. Furthermore, I believe in bringing a songlist to the worship experience. Worship leaders should prepare a list in advance, review and rehearse it with their worship team, and bring it to the worship gathering. Some people may think that we can flow in worship more easily if we have no preconceived ideas of what direction the worship may take; in my experience, this kind of open-ended absence of prayerful premeditation does not help us find the river but usually sends us wandering in a wasteland of aimlessness.

The preparation of a songlist and the rehearsal of those songs equip us to move forward with purpose toward the river of God. In no way should anything in this book be interpreted as a negative slant toward the pivotal importance of preparation. However, there is a profound tension between preparing for a worship service and then having the flexibility to flow spontaneously with the river of God. I'm advocating for both.

Equipping The Workbench

When a worship team practices and masters a new song, they are expanding their repertoire and can now draw upon that song at will. In so doing, it's like a skilled mechanic who adds a new, specialized tool to his workbench. Every tool he adds to his collection means he is better equipped to service a wider spectrum of customer's needs.

Every new song learned is like a new tool. It has a unique role it can fulfill in worship because of its particular lyrics and the distinctive mood the song evokes. The broader our range of musical styles and lyrical content, the more equipped we are to flow with the river of God once we find it.

However, once we get into the flow of worship and find the river of God, we must be ready to think outside the box of our preparation. Some worship leaders are insistent that the songs we practiced in our Thursday night rehearsal be sung on Sunday morning. It really doesn't work exactly like that. Let me illustrate.

You take your car to the shop for an oil change. When you pick your car up later, you discover the mechanic has aligned your tires instead. You say, "I didn't need my tires aligned. I needed an oil change!" So the mechanic says, "They've been teaching us all week how to align tires, so that's what we're practicing on every car that comes in today."

Obviously that's ludicrous. But that's what many worship leaders do on Sunday mornings. "Our worship team practiced this song, we worked real hard on it, we took our entire Thursday evening to get this song mastered—so you *will* learn it! And you will like it!" It doesn't matter if the song contributes to finding the river; we've practiced the song so we're going to sing it.

Listen: Just because you practiced the song doesn't mean it's the right song for Sunday morning. Bring it to the meeting, have it ready to introduce, but then hold the song lightly with an open hand. If the Lord begins to take the meeting in a direction you didn't anticipate, be willing to postpone the new song for another time. God's river has a way of taking us in directions we hadn't expected.

Some worship leaders sometimes have a tiny bit of an agenda to fit a certain song into a meeting. Perhaps it's a song they themselves have written, and so singing the song can give exposure to their ministry. Leaders need to have a greater passion for the river than anything else. If the song doesn't contribute to moving in the immediate river, let's postpone it to another meeting.

Preparation empowers you to deviate from your preparation. Preparation is not confining but releasing. Your songlist is like your boat. When you have a songlist that has been rehearsed and is ready to go, you have a safety net you can always fall back on. Having the songlist gives you the courage to step out of the boat and walk on water. You know you can always swim back to your songlist. It's preparation that gives us the courage to step into the unknown that the river represents.

Getting The Right Blend

In my opinion, a good *vacation* is the right blend between planning and spontaneity. Some people plan their vacations down to every hour of every day. They may do a lot of stuff, but they have no room for the delight of spontaneity. Others, on the other hand, don't plan anything for their vacation and they often end up doing just that—nothing. So my angle on it is this: Plan your vacation but leave flexibility in your plans for things impetuous.

I'm also of the opinion that a good *date* is the right blend between planning and spontaneity. Put some energy into planning the date so there's a skeleton plan of what you're going to do—a movie, a stroll in the park, a nice restaurant, whatever. But leave room in your plans to change direction on a whim and scamper down some unforeseen adventure. That's often where the delight of romance is to be found.

Similarly, I believe that a good *worship experience* is the right blend between planning and spontaneity. Planning is essential; but the greatest heights of worship are usually found by flowing spontaneously with the river of God.

Take an illustration from the world of jazz. Kansas City, where we live, developed a reputation several decades ago for being a hotbed for experimental jazz. The symphony would come to town, and then after the performance the symphony musicians would sneak down to Vine Street where they would take in the adventure of one of the city's jazz clubs. Back in those days, the jazz band would have a spare sax or trumpet or some such instrument on the platform, and folks from the audience could come up and try their hand at jousting with the band. When the symphony players showed up, the contest began. Who could shake whom? They would start with a jazz riff that had a pattern to it and then move out on the waters of improvisation. The band would try to lose and humiliate the trained symphony players. Moving out into the spontaneous in jazz was a walk on the wild side, and it was exhilarating to see how far out there one could get without drowning.

Inherent to jazz is the understanding that it starts with a well-established musical pattern, but finds its greatest impetus when the edges become blurred and the boundaries of what is possible are pushed and pressed to their maximum extension.

I saw a jazz documentary on TV once that ended with this profound quip: "Life is a lot like jazz: It's best when you improvise." The same is true in worship. Structure and preparation are valuable, but the glory of God's river is best discovered when we step out of the boat of our preparation and become engaged with the Lord Jesus in the spontaneous passions of the moment.

Here's my advice: Prepare a list—then go river-hunting.

Beyond Preparation

Worship must transcend preparation. If it doesn't, all we have is a "song service." A song service is a list of songs, sung one after the other in a linear fashion, until the time runs out.

"Oh, I love that song!" So we cut and paste the song into our songlist. "This new CD from England has a fantastic single on it." Cut, paste. "This worship song from Australia is tremendous!" Cut, paste. "And let's not forget this new title from Vineyard." Cut, paste. "I love the black gospel sound of this new CD out of Atlanta." Cut, paste. So we take the worship expressions from a variety of worshipers from all over the place, string the songs together into a songlist, sing them one after the other on Sunday morning, and call it a worship service. No, that's not a worship service; that's a song service.

It's not a worship service until you find the river.

As long as you're singing somebody else's worship, it's just another song. It doesn't become worship until something happens in the depths of your own spirit.

To have a worship service, you must transcend songs. For a song service to become a worship service, a shift must happen at a spiritual level. A threshold into God's presence must be crossed. Something alive and pulsating must be found within the hearts of God's people. It's not worship until we move past the songs and encounter God.

A Time For Everything

I travel to quite a few churches, and I'm surprised at how many worship teams will use the last 15 minutes before the service to fine-tune their musical grip on the meeting's songs. They'll practice their intro a couple more times, or tighten some three-part harmonies on the chorus, or make sure the bass player is playing the right inversions on the chord progression. But I just want to say to them, "You're missing the point."

We're agreed that what we all want is the river. We're not going to find the river, however, by having tighter harmonies and a cleaner bass line. What will take us to the river? "'Not by might nor by power, but by My Spirit,' says the LORD of hosts" (Zechariah 4:6). The river is a God thing. No amount of practice can produce the river. So bottom line, prayer is more important than practice.

There is a time to practice. Set aside an evening in the week for the worship team to rehearse. But when you're just moments before service starting time, that's the time to be digging wells in the Spirit. That's the time to be reaching out in intercession and passion. That's the time to tune our hearts to His heart. When a worship team owns the reality of John 15:5, "'Without Me you can do nothing,'" then we will use the spare moments before the worship service to lean with all our hearts upon our Beloved. He alone can take us to the river.

CHAPTER Six

Leading Worship Or Leading Songs?

As said in the previous chapter, there is a difference between a worship service and a song service. It's the same difference that exists between a musician and what I call a "copyist."

Musician Versus Copyist

A copyist is someone who has learned how to copy true musicians. We teach kids from their childhood to be copyists. We put the sheet on the music stand; then we teach them that when they see a certain note on the sheet, they should depress a certain key on the piano. See the note; play the note. See the next note; play the next note. We teach them to practice until they can transpose all the notes on the sheet through their minds, through their fingers, and into the instrument. And *voilà*—out comes music! It sounds just as beautiful as when the original musician composed the piece.

Eventually these students become so proficient at reproducing sheet music that we glibly call them musicians. But they're not musicians; they're copyists. They haven't even begun to enter into the incubating process that the original musician experienced when he or she first wrote the music.

Copyists are like courtroom stenographers. Their job is to reproduce what is coming to them with impeccable accuracy. Copyists are also like people employed in data entry. If you have a job in data entry, you'll get fired for being creative. In the same way, we have castigated young would-be musicians for getting creative with their music. If they deviated from the written music with the slightest hint of creativity, they got their knuckles rapped. "That's not how the song was written! Play the music as it's written!" So we've actually taught young people to shut down their creative juices and learn to simply reproduce what's on the page.

Copyists reproduce copyists. Many of our music schools are staffed by copyists, and they in turn train up other copyists. Some music schools would be better called mimic schools.

I remember interviewing a woman once for a job in our music program, who came highly recommended and well laureled. She had the equivalent of a doctoral degree in music. I was impressed by her dexterity on the piano. I said to her, "Just play a worship song, any song you like." She said, "Which song?" I said, "You choose." She said, "Well, give me a sheet." I said, "No, no sheet. Just play something. Just make music." She got a panicked look in her eyes. "Give me a sheet," she pleaded. "No," I said, "I don't want you to play from notes; I just want you to create some music here on the spot." She turned pale and began to fumble around the keyboard like a lost lamb. I felt so badly for her. She had been trained to be a master copyist, but no one had helped her to make the transition to become a musician herself.

I consider this a travesty. Young people are going

to music schools and spending multiplied thousands of dollars, only to be trained up as copyists by other trained copyists. We call them musicians because they know how to reproduce the same sounds that the composing musicians made.

I do not mean to sound disparaging toward trained copyists. There are many church contexts where we are grateful for those who read music. Furthermore, I know of many copyists who are exercising themselves wonderfully to become producers of music themselves. I am simply saying that any system which produces only copyists needs to be challenged with a higher vision.

A copyist works from the head; a musician works from the heart. For a musician, music starts down in the gut. In the intestinal region. Music starts as a feeling, a mood, an emotion, a sentiment, a fire. A musician feels his music. He emotes the notes. His music begins as a churning of the soul, extends through his mind, projects through his fingers, and comes out of the instrument with a soul all its own. It is a transmitting of passion from the medium of the heart to the medium of the art. For a musician, it's like giving birth to a baby. When the music is manifest, it is an extension of his very soul. This is why musicians take critiques of their music so personally; if you criticize their music, they reckon you're criticizing *them*.

Song Service Versus Worship Service

Now take the above illustration—the distinction between a musician and a copyist—and see it as the same difference between a worship service and a song service. Just as a copyist analytically reproduces someone else's music, a song service is the replication of other people's worship songs, sung one after the other. And just as a musician makes music from an inner creative cauldron, a worship service finds its impetus from an inner furnace of love that burns in the hearts of God's people and is fueled from the altar in heaven. A song service keeps everyone's minds engaged; a worship service engages the hearts.

A worship service has a life of its own. It's a heart to heart, spirit to spirit encounter with God. Something powerful begins to formulate in the procreative womb of corporate worship. It produces a worship experience with a clear identity and thematic thrust. There is a travail and a bringing to birth. Something begins to stir in the inward parts (Psalm 51:6). Deep calls unto deep (Psalm 42:7). The spirit within man begins to respond to the initiatives of the Holy Spirit, as He woos us and draws us forward into passion. Love begins to be awakened.

The impetus for the song is finding its origination in the spirit within, not from the music without. Something alive in the midst of the congregation is fighting to reach an external expression. The love of God is permeating the human spirit and soul (Romans 5:5), and it begins to erupt in a self-regenerating flow of heartfelt worship to the Lover of our souls (John 7:38).

When a song service transitions into a worship service, there is a collective movement from our minds to our hearts. Something organic begins to take place. Suddenly the worship time begins to coalesce and take shape as a living, breathing, growing, flowing entity. It pulsates with its own synergism and vitality. It carries its own unique momentum that is carried along by the bubbling waters of the Holy Spirit. Once it gains a head of steam, it finds a life all of its own. It becomes a holy dance of intimate affection that nobody wants to squelch prematurely lest they be guilty of touching the ark of God (see the story of Uzzah in 2 Samuel 6:1-10). It deserves the dignity of coming to mature expression and then finding its own completion.

A Story

On one occasion, I was invited to speak at a worship conference where an internationally known songwriter and worship leader was also on the list of guest ministers. I was excited at the opportunity to hear this brother in person. He was going to be leading an entire evening of worship, and I was so looking forward to the meeting. This brother has an incredible anointing on his songwriting, his songs are sung around the world, and it's obvious that he has a living worship connection in his heart with the Lord. I couldn't wait to taste of it in person.

When the meeting launched, the dear brother led us in a song service! He had taken a bunch of the songs he had written, listed them in a certain order, and proceeded to move through his list of his own original songs. There is no doubt in my mind that when he first wrote the songs, they were written in the flow of the river of God. But now, as we were moving through them one after the other, the river was not to be found. We were in a good, old-fashioned song service.

It seemed to me that the brother had not made the transition. He knew what it was to get in his secret place with God, enter into the womb of worship, and allow the procreative juices of true worship to stir his heart and produce genuine expressions of worship. His songs were equipping the international church! But when he stepped onto the platform, instead of finding that same place of gestation and incubation and abiding love relationship with the Lord Jesus, he reverted to simply singing the songs he had written.

God deliver us of songlist services. As the Bride of Christ gathers together to give her love to her Lord, may we never settle for anything less than the living reality of a vibrant love connection with Jesus.

CHAPTER Seven

Weaving A Glorious Tapestry

S o now, let me ask you a question. Why shouldn't I just stay home when the church is gathering together, plug in a worship CD, and worship the Lord privately in my home? After all, there are some great worship CDs available these days, and I can get better quality music out of my CD player than I get when I go to the congregation. So why go to church? Why not stay home and worship with the CD?

Here's one reason: *CDs follow straight lines.* CDs go through their songs one after the other—boom, boom, boom. You'll never find the river with your CD player. You may get blessed a bit, but you'll not swim in the waters of the Ezekiel 47 river. To find the river, you've got to move past the linear movement of a CD and get into the flowing, creative waters of corporate worship.

CD Syndrome

The levels of musicianship in the body of Christ have improved dramatically in the past 25 years. If you were to rent a time machine and take a trip back to your average worship service in America 20 or 25 years ago, you would experience culture shock. The levels of musicianship were a far cry from what they are today. What is to account for this phenomenal acceleration in the church's musical expressions of recent years?

The answer, I'm convinced, is Integrity's Hosanna Music. And Vineyard Music. And Maranatha! Music. And Hillsong. And Worship Together. And a number of other worship CD-producing companies.

Here's what happened. People would turn on the worship CD in their car on their way to church, and the whole car would be swaying from side to side as the passengers would jive to the music and participate in the joy of the excellent recording. Then, they'd step into church and get depressed at the dysfunctional mess on the platform. Then, they'd step back into their cars and jive all the way home.

The worship leaders were in for a rude wake-up call. "Hey," they finally realized, "we're competing with the CD!" So somebody said, "Maybe we should practice." The worship ministries of our nation began to practice just to save face before the people. The Lord honored it, and the level of musicianship in most churches began to skyrocket. Pretty soon many worship teams were able to keep pace with the CDs that were coming out.

But now we have another problem in the church, a problem that I call "a CD syndrome." The quality of worship is so polished and smooth in many of our churches that you could actually record Sunday morning worship and sell the CDs! The intros are tight, the modulations are smooth, the harmonies are impeccable, the musicianship is flawless, the segues are impressive, and the endings are a work of art.

With just one problem. I don't come to church for CD-quality music. If I wanted CD-quality music, I would stay home and play the CD. I come to church for something totally different. I come to the house of God because I want to enter into the divine dance, into a breathing, living, dynamic love exchange between the Bridegroom and the Bride. I come to the house of prayer because *I want the river!*

We assemble with God's people because we don't want to miss the glories of the river of God. We never know when we'll hit the river, so we'll keep coming week after week, taking our chances and risking disappointment. "Not today. Oh well. Maybe next time." So we keep coming back to the place of corporate worship, hoping it will happen. Hoping we'll touch a little of heaven on earth. Hoping we'll find the river. We avoid being absent because we don't want to be like the apostle Thomas on Resurrection Day—Jesus showed up to the meeting, but he was too busy or distracted to be there. When Jesus shows up I want to be there! So I'll hazard a thousand disappointments, if need be, in order to be present when the glory of God thunders loose in the midst of God's people.

The Tapestry Of Worship

Each event of congregational worship is an unreplicated, one-of-a-kind, never-been-seen-before-in-the-history-of-the-planet, never-to-be-seen-again, breathing love exchange with our Beloved. Why? Because never before, in the history of the world, has this specific group of people gathered together in this way, with all their existing mindsets, attitudes, and the emotional trappings of their current life issues. So when we express ourselves together before the throne of God, the nature and themes of our expressions will be different from any other worship service that has ever transpired. When this group of saints touches the heart of God, a tapestry of worship will begin to emerge that will be absolutely unique in its emphasis and flavor.

Every worship service is like the on-site formation of a new tapestry. Together we are producing something that is unique, living, immediate, and fresh. When the service starts, nobody knows how the tapestry will end. But as we enter the river of God, out of the synergism of corporate worship begins to emerge a tapestry of affection that glitters and shines with compelling beauty.

The emphasis, tone, and direction of every worship service is totally unique. If we'll allow the worship time to come to it's completion, we will come away with a clear awareness of having received His love, having given Him our love, and having been empowered to go out into the world through His enabling grace. When worship's tapesty is finished, everyone comes away with a clear understanding of what the Spirit is saying to the church.

For the tapestry of corporate worship to be complete, we need *everybody's* thread. To the degree that some people's thread is absent due to passivity, to that degree the corporate worship experience falls short of its potential fullness.

- The worship leader must contribute his or her thread. If the worship leader is too confined to the songlist, and is too intimidated to step out of the boat and go with the river of God, the tapestry of worship will fall short.

- The pastors and elders must lend their threads. If they're thinking, "I'm off duty; it's the worship leader's turn," then they will not be leaning into the Spirit for that contribution that their threads might make.

- We need the threads from the singers on the worship team. If they're telling themselves, "I don't have a prophetic anointing on my life, so I'm just going to sing the songs as they've been written," then we will miss what could have been. Listen to me, all you singers in the house of God: You have a prophetic anointing! Whether you're totally comfortable with it or not, God has called you to prophesy in song in the courts of the Lord (1 Samuel 10:5-6). If the insecurities of your flesh are winning out, then repent, take out your thread, and weave your part of the tapestry.

* The prophetic musicians have a thread to weave. "But I'm not prophetic," complains a musician. Sorry, it's too late. God has already anointed you to play your instrument under a prophetic anointing (1 Chronicles 25:1). With the calling came the grace to fulfill that calling. Prophetic singers and musicians, you often face a choice: either play it safe and stay back in the shallows of your comfort zones or launch out into a prophetic anointing that takes us over our heads in the river. If you hold back, you rob us of what could have been.

* And last but not least, the congregation has the greatest contribution to make to the tapestry. Each saint has his or her own thread. If any believers are disengaged or withdrawn, their threads will be greatly missed, and we will never enter into the full reality of what we could have experienced in the river of God. For the tapestry to be complete, we need everyone's thread!

Because of this dynamic, today's worship leaders display a lower personal profile and a more open hand than their predecessors. They realize they must provide on-ramps for others to make their contribution to the worship service, which is often done by affording brief moments of pause in their leadership of the worship service. By displaying a lower profile, worship leaders allow the Holy Spirit to bring impetus to the meeting through other members in the congregation or worship team upon whom He is moving.

Corporate worship is so much more than a slick display of CD-quality music. It is a breathing love-exchange with the Bridegroom in which every member contributes his or her part. When Jesus contributes His part, worship then becomes an explosive encounter with a holy God. Before us is the potential to have such a clear and compelling meeting with God that we all remember it vividly for days—the emphasis of the tapesty etched clearly upon our minds, and our hearts empowered to respond more freely and fully to Him in obedience and love.

We won't be satisfied until our corporate worship times become unforgettable tapestries that are woven in the unpredictable fluidity of the Holy Spirit's river.

CHAPTER Eight

Worship Wars

There's a Civil War in the church today over worship. There may be no area of ministry in the church that receives more complaints and carries more controversy than the ministry of worship. If one group is happy, you can almost be guaranteed the other group is not.

To clarify, the war is not between the Pentecostals and the Baptists, nor between the Wesleyans and the Presbyterians, nor between pipe organs and guitars, nor between Rock music and Country music. Do you want to know where the battle lines are actually drawn? *The war is between the old song and the new song.*

The Beauty Of the Old

The old song is vital to true worship, carrying with it some tremendous qualities like:

- Stability: The old song has proven its ability to endure the erosion of time and to withstand the furor of storms.

- Continuity: The old song enables today's three

generations to join together in glorifying God with one voice.

* Vocabulary: The old song has proven its ability to articulate precious truths of the faith.

* Historicity: The old song roots us to the rich heritage of our forefathers, connecting us to our corporate identity as the multi-generational church of God.

* Orthodoxy: The old song gives us language to celebrate the creeds and proven theologies of the church.

* Safety: The old song provides security and comfort, largely because it is familiar.

* Satisfaction: The old song is so satiating to the soul that once you've had the old, you don't want the new, for you say, "The old is better" (see Luke 5:39).

The Role of New and Old

The old song plays a crucial role in the worship life of the church, and yet when all we have is the old, our tendency is to back off from contending for the new thing God is always doing in the earth (Isaiah 43:19).

When we settle for only the old song, we enjoy all the above benefits, but there is one lacking dimension. There is one thing the new song supplies that is generally lacking in the old—power. The new song provides power. It's possible occasionally to have a powerful worship service with just the old song, but it's the exception. In the vast majority of instances, the unthrottled power of worship is tapped and unlocked in the new song.

There is a "breaker anointing" that sometimes attends

the new song. Micah 2:13 describes the breaker anointing, which is a grace from heaven to break through barriers and move God's people into the next dimension of Kingdom living. While not every new song will always have that barrier-breaking quality, your chances of finding that kind of breakthrough are best when you move into the new song.

Or, to use the language of Ephesians 5:19, psalms and hymns may pull everyone together and take you to the river, but it's the spiritual songs (new songs) that will take you down the river into the swimming depths.

I'm not saying the new song is always powerful. I've been in plenty of worship gatherings where a lot of new songs were sung and there was no power in the meeting at all. The new song has as much potential to fall flat as does the old song. However, when the Spirit is breathing upon our worship, it's the new song that has the ability to transform the spiritual landscape.

On the positive side, the power of worship is in the new song. On the down side, the new song often seems volatile, unpredictable, raucous, and disruptive. Like the new wine, it foments in a swirl of energy that can be explosive and unsettling to those who want to be able to predict every move in advance.

Obviously there are trade-offs. At some point we need to decide whether we're willing to hazard the volatile nature of the new song in order to enjoy its benefits. If we have the courage to navigate the bumps, the new song has the power to catapult us forward into our destiny in God.

What Is the "New Song"?

When I speak of "the new song," I am thinking of two primary categories:

- A song that is new to our church. When a song is first introduced to our worshiping community, it's a new song to us regardless of when it was written. The song may be 100 years old, but if we've never heard or sung it before, it's new in our book. One kind of new song that is especially fitting is a song that is newly written by a congregation member. Perhaps someone within the house is able to capture precisely what the Holy Spirit has been saying to our fellowship in recent days and to express that theme creatively through a new composition.

- A song that has never been sung before. Here's where the new song really gets interesting. When the river of God begins to flow in a meeting, and the worshipers are getting caught up in the glory and refreshment of the living waters, something begins to happen within the hearts of worshipers. They begin to have a new song rise up from within, begging for expression. We appreciate the lyrics that songwriters give us, but when we're in the river, our worship surges over the banks of pre-written lyrics and published hymns. Suddenly we find ourselves wanting to express a song of the moment, a song that comes directly from the heart of a lovesick worshiper. It probably won't rhyme, and it may not have a smooth meter to it, but it's fresh and passionate and alive. We've never sung it quite like this before, and we probably never will ever again, because it's a "now" song that expresses our immediate heart cry. And it's powerful!

In Romans 7:6, Paul speaks of "the newness of the Spirit," which he contrasts with "the oldness of the letter." His point is that the Spirit is ever new. Where the Spirit of the Lord is active, there's always something new stirring. So when the Holy Spirit takes hold of our worship, He is always generating new songs in the hearts of the faithful. Spirit-led worship will have a "newness" to it. (If you don't have newness in your worship, get stir crazy.) When you hit the river you can't help it—a new song just automatically flows.

New and Old In Heaven

In heaven, they're singing both the new song and the old song. Revelation 15:3 tells us they're singing the song of Moses in heaven; well, that song is a few thousand years old. But there's an even older song in heaven. It's recorded for us in Revelation 4:8—"'Holy, holy, holy, Lord God Almighty, who was and is and is to come!'" That song is older than the hills. It has been sung around the throne of God for many millions of years. So in heaven they appreciate the old song.

But they also sing the new song in heaven.

> Now when He had taken the scroll, the four living creatures and the twenty-four elders fell down before the Lamb, each having a harp, and golden bowls full of incense, which are the prayers of the saints. *And they sang a new song,* saying: "You are worthy to take the scroll, and to open its seals; for You were slain, and have redeemed us to God by Your blood out of every tribe and tongue and people and nation" (Revelation 5:8-9.

If they're singing songs both new and old in heaven's

river, and we're praying for God's will to be accomplished on earth as it is in heaven, wouldn't it be reasonable to conclude that we should be singing both new and old songs in the church of Jesus here on earth? The wise worship leader will bring out of his or her storehouse songs new and old (see Matthew 13:52).

The Skill of Juggling Both

The old song unites people together in one common, familiar expression that enables them to flow together in momentum as a group. When an old song is pulled out, watch the room draw together.

Then, when we lead out in a new song, the dynamics change. People are somewhat hesitant because they're not sure where this new song is going. So when a new song is first thrown out, it can have the effect initially of appearing to dissipate the momentum of the meeting. To rally everyone again, an old song may need to follow a new song. But once the new song "takes," it will have a kind of anointing on it that is richer and stronger than that of the old song.

Worship leaders who are enthusiastic to see the release of the new song sometimes make the mistake of devoting too much time to new songs—and the overall momentum of the meeting can suffer as a result. They love the new, but don't always discern when the congregation has become disengaged and distant. When that happens, what can a worship leader do to get those who have drifted off mentally to become engaged again in what's happening? Usually the best solution is to come back to an old song.

Worship gatherings that flow with the river of God usually are led with wisdom and expertise by a leader who knows how to use the old song to draw a room together in cohesiveness, then use the new song to release a surge of energy and power. But when the energy level dissipates, the leader knows to return to the old song. The river is best followed by alternating wisely between the old and the new song. Effective leaders have learned the dance of balancing between the two.

The old song gathers; the new song propels. The old song unites us so we can flow together; the new song has the power to catapult us into deeper waters. Instead of pitting one against the other, let's maximize both. If we do, we have the best chance of finding and following the river.

CHAPTER Nine

Grateful Dead

When we speak of worship being an organic entity that finds its own energy in the dynamism of the river, or when we speak of flowing gracefully between the new and the old song, an example comes to mind that I hope will be helpful. I want to illustrate this from the experiences of a non-Christian rock band. Stay with me, I think you'll find this example quite illuminating.

One of the most fascinating advents of the rock-n-roll era has been the uncommon legacy of an American band called "The Grateful Dead." The driving force of the band was guitarist Jerry Garcia, who led the band with his innovative chord sequences and colorful harmonics. The group toured regularly from the late 1960's until Garcia's death in 1995.

The band would go through their customary songs during their concerts but then at some point would shift gears. Turning from their prepared repertoire, they would launch out into an improvisational riff, find a groove that was working musically, and then begin to push the envelope. The drummer would throw in unusual syncopations; the guitars would whine and scream creatively; the keyboard would strain for color and dissonance. Together, they would move out to the edge of almost losing one another musically, but yet would follow each other's improvisational initiatives closely enough so that they stayed together. And then they would begin to grope for "it."

"It" was what would sometimes happen in the midst of one of these improvisational free-for-alls. Occasionally, the band would catch a wave of momentum, an emotional energy would ripple through the auditorium, a power would grip both the band members and the audience, and the concert would take off into another dimension. They had found "it."

When this happened—whatever it was—the concert hall became an explosive altar of spiritual encounter. Everybody in the place knew that a line had been crossed, the transition had been made, and now the night became a pulsating celebration of connectedness to a cosmic consciousness. It became unclear whether the band or the audience was leading, as the concert became a participatory dance that included every attendee. It was spirit, and it was palpably real.

The spiritual atmosphere that filled the concerts was so powerfully compelling, in fact, that many fans became spiritual followers, actually making the Grateful Dead their religion. They called themselves Dead Heads. Garcia was viewed by many as their spiritual leader and came to be dubbed "the godfather," a term he privately disliked. Fans would get in their Volkswagen vans and follow the band from city to city, reserving their place in one concert after another. If it didn't happen in one concert—that is, if they didn't cross the spiritual threshold—then they would just pick up and go to the next one, knowing that eventually it would happen again.

Once the transition was made in a concert, a spiritual energy would actually take over. It was as though the band members could read each other's minds. They instinctively knew where the others were going, what song would be sung next, or what the next chord was going to be. The power on the stage was intoxicating as the band held the hearts of multiplied thousands in their hands.

One former Dead Head told me that when the concert would crescendo, the crowd would empty their pockets and begin to share what they had with one another. Quite often it would be some form of a drug, but the fact remains that a generosity would overtake the crowd. I was also told that when the throngs would eventually leave the stadium, they would shuffle out quietly except that they would bleat like sheep.

My Personal Amazement

When I first learned about what happened in these concerts, I was totally fascinated. Having grown up in a Christian family, I never went to a secular concert of any kind during my growing up years, much less a Grateful Dead concert. So I had no idea what happened at such events. I knew what it was like to be in a Christian meeting and have a holy anointing take hold of a worship service, but I had no idea there was a counterfeit anointing that operated in a similar way at secular concerts. So I wanted to learn more about this dynamic.

A friend of mine used to play guitar in a variety of bands during his younger, pre-Christ years, and he told me all the bands of the day would look to the Grateful Dead as their role model. They would all try to find the same kind of improvisational groove and spiritual momentum, but they couldn't ever reach quite the same plateau for some reason.

Now, I have a bit of a confession to make. I'm not proud
of this, but it's the truth. It really happened to me. Back in
the 1970's, when I was going through some of my teenage
crisis years, I went through about a five-year period when
I listened regularly to Top 40 Radio. Ouch, now the truth
is out. So if the song was a hit in the 70's, I probably knew
the song.

So as they're telling me the story of the Grateful Dead,
I'm scrolling back to my recollections of 1970's rock-n-roll.
"Grateful Dead...Grateful Dead...let me think. What was a
song on the radio by Grateful Dead?" And I couldn't think
of a single Top 40 hit performed by that group.

That's when I was told, "The Grateful Dead didn't
have any hits." Apparently they had no hit albums, nor
hit singles. The power of the band was not in their ability
to produce hits but was rather in the power of their live
concerts. (Imagine my surprise to learn they were the
number one top grossing rock-n-roll band in the world for
at least 30 years, even without a single hit album.)

For that reason, there is an active internet industry,
up to the present day, of fans who sell or swap recordings
of concerts that reach back 35 or more years. The band
had the policy of allowing fans to bring portable cassette
recorders into the concerts, so as a result there are a host
of homemade recordings that are still being duplicated
and sold between fans worldwide. The Grateful Dead did
produce some studio recordings, but that's not primarily
what the fans want. The greatest demand remains for
the low-fidelity, home-spun recordings that carry the
unpolished, spontaneous ambience of the live concerts.

The Other River

One reason I was so fascinated by these accounts of
their concerts was because I had no idea, growing up in my

Christian world, that there was an unholy river. I knew there was a holy river of God to be found in worship, but I had no idea that Satan, the master counterfeiter, had devised a way to harness the power of music to sweep the hearts of the undiscerning into a river that leads to death.

When this river began to take over the concerts, Mickey Hart (one of the band members) coined a term to describe what was happening. He would say, "It's when the seventh man shows up." So I asked my friends what he meant by that term. Apparently there were six people in the band at the time he coined the phrase. He was recognizing that there was a power present in the concert that went beyond the members of the band. There was a spiritual presence which gave to the band an impact that exceeded the sum of the parts.

The Grateful Dead had found the river—the other river—and used it to promote their own agenda. But I will say this to their credit: They discovered more of what God intended through music than have most churches today. It is here that the saying applies, "'I will provoke them to jealousy by those who are not a nation'" (Deuteronomy 32:21). We who have the right to the great river of God stay back in the shallows of our rigid service orders and miss the fullest purpose for which God created music.

The Fourth Man

My point in this chapter is not to talk about The Grateful Dead *per se*. The point I want to make is that where there is the counterfeit, it is testimony to the existence of the genuine. The experiences of a secular band only serve to substantiate that there is a reality that is available to us in God—a river of divine glory that can be touched in corporate worship.

When they touched their river, they described it as "when the seventh man shows up." But when we touch our river, I prefer to call it "when the Fourth Man shows up."

I'm referring to the time when Nebuchadnezzar threw the three Hebrew slaves into his fiery furnace, but when he looked into the flame, he saw not only three men walking around, but also the form of a Fourth in the fire (read Daniel 3). And the Fourth looked like the Son of God—because that's who He was!

There is a fiery river to be found in God, and when we find it, it is a blazing inferno in which the Fourth Man, Jesus Christ, reveals Himself. In this fire, bondages are burned away. (The ropes were burned off the hands of the Hebrew men.) In this fire, there are manifestations of the Glory of God. There are healings and miracles; there is power to be delivered from demonic snares; there is a holy anointing that causes unbelievers to fall on their face in conviction, to confess their sins, and to leave the meeting saying, "If you go to that place, you will meet up with God!" (1 Corinthians 14:25).

Oh God, evermore give us these waters to drink!

CHAPTER Ten

Sea of Glass Worship

N ow let me tell you what you really want: You want sea of glass worship (Revelation 4:6; 15:2). You've got heaven in your heart (Ecclesiastes 3:11). You can't help yourself; this desire has been infused into your soul by God. You long to stand on the great sea of glass, in glory, gazing upon the throne of God Almighty, His fire flowing into your spirit, setting you on fire with God-sized passions for the face of Jesus Christ, your love now flowing back to Him in gratitude and exhilaration. For this you were created. Nothing less will ever fully satisfy you.

When John saw sea of glass worship, here's his description.

> After these things I looked, and behold, a great multitude which no one could number, of all nations, tribes, peoples, and tongues, standing before the throne and before the Lamb, clothed with white robes, with palm branches in their hands, and crying out with a loud voice, saying, "Salvation belongs to our God who sits on the throne, and to the Lamb!" (Revelation 7:9-10).

Notice, first of all, that John saw a *great multitude.* The worship of heaven is multitude-driven. In contrast, contemporary worship on earth tends to be platform-driven. So the fullness of heaven's worship stands in stark contrast to our typical worship services.

I sometimes wonder what John might have written if he had been caught up in the Spirit to one of our worship services, instead of to heaven's worship service. The differences would have been almost humorous.

> "And I, John, beheld, and lo, a platform. And on the platform, a microphone. And at the microphone, a leader. And slightly behind the leader were four singers, each with a microphone. And the leader's microphone was louder than theirs. And lo, I saw a keyboard. And guitars. And a drumset. And speakers. And the sound coming from the platform was so powerful that you couldn't tell if anyone was singing."

Please understand, that even as I'm having us laugh at ourselves a little bit, I am not critical of contemporary worship. I know we're all doing the best we know to do. My point is, I simply want to highlight one of the primary differences between heaven's worship and our worship today. Heaven's worship is multitude-driven; our worship is platform-driven. To be successful, contemporary worship relies heavily upon the role of leaders and musicians to take us from commencement to completion.

When you look at the heavenly scenes of Revelation, you'll notice there's one thing curiously absent from heaven's worship—a worship leader! That's because they don't need a worship leader in heaven. They don't need someone to be saying, "Everyone lift your hands," or, "Let me hear you sing it," or, "Worship the Lord with your entire being." Because when you're standing on the sea of glass, and the river of fire is pouring into your spirit, you don't need someone reminding you to stay engaged in worshiping the Lord; you *are* engaged! You've got a river springing up from within; you're beholding the very throne and face of God; waves of glory are emanating from the throne and igniting your heart; and you are surrounded by burning ones. You've never felt so alive in all your life. You are drinking of eternal life! You've finally made it to the worship service where you don't need someone to prod you to worship. That's because the river *is* the worship leader.

The Great Hindrance

If we are to experience sea of glass worship—worship on earth as it is in heaven—there is one great obstacle that must be overcome and transformed. Not that it's the only hindrance, by any means, but in my judgment it's foremost. *The most powerful hindrance to heavenly worship being experienced today is the general passivity of your typical congregation.*

Please don't take me wrong—I'm not angry at anyone. I'm simply trying to bring the issues into the light so we can deal with them openly and move toward God's best.

I've asked myself the question, "Why are most congregations passive in their worship participation, looking to the platform to provide the direction and impetus for worship?" The answer is probably complex and varied, with the following being only a sampling of the manifold reasons:

- For many, the issue is timidity. It's not that they mean to be rebellious and resistant to the Spirit's flow in worship. Rather, they are like doves hiding in fear or uncertainty. This is why our Beloved so frequently beckons to us, "'O my dove, in the clefts of the rock, in the secret places of the clff, let me see your face, let me hear your voice; for your voice is sweet, and your face is lovely'" (Song of Solomon 2:14). He longs to assure us that we can lift our faces and voices with boldness in His presence because we've been given the right to be children of God (John 1:12).

* Some worshipers come to the meeting with hearts that are spiritually cool and somewhat disconnected from God. They want to connect with God and step into the river, but they rely on the platform ministry to help them get there.

* Some worshipers participate in worship in direct proportion to how they enjoy the leadership style on the platform. If they like the way the worship team is leading, they will engage; if they don't enjoy the leadership style, they instinctively pull back.

* Since the worship of virtually all our churches is platform-driven, a lot of believers have never even stopped to question our methodology. They simply accept the fact that it's the worship team's job to try to get the people to open up. A stylistic preference has evolved into a cultural norm.

* In many facilities, the acoustics and architecture of the building are designed strategically for the platform to provide leadership and the multitude to follow.

* People want to conduct themselves in an orderly manner in church, so they slip into a mode of responding in meekness to the directives coming from the platform.

Many believers have never caught a vision for contending for anything more than a paradigm in which the few on the platform are fully engaged and proactive, while the many in the congegation are splayed into a wide spectrum that ranges from zeal to stupor. If I do nothing else with this book, I intend to place a vision before you that beckons, "There's more!"

The Great Multitude

On the sea of glass, the great multitude is 100% proactively engaged in worship. There is no need for anyone to exhort them to wake up because a river of fire is flowing into their hearts by the power of the Holy Spirit, causing each member of the Bride of Christ to erupt with extravagant affections for the beloved Bridegroom. On the sea of glass, the great multitude has *ownership* of the worship. Nothing can extinguish their flame.

To contend for the same dynamic in our worship services, congregations must rise to their identity as "the great multitude." That's who we are! We stand on the sea of glass—we really do! We are not able to see it the same way we will see one day; but if the veil were removed from our eyes, we would be stunned to realize that we stand on the sea of glass even now in our congregations, with our eyes on the throne, and our hearts set ablaze by the fire that flows from God's throne. The only difference between then and now is that we still live with the veil over our eyes. But even though we can't see, it doesn't change the fact that we stand before God's throne even now, because of the precious blood of Christ, and burn before the throne of God with God-empowered passions and affections.

We are the great multitude! We stand before God! We burn with holy fire! We don't need a worship leader to jump-start us or a worship team to direct our every word because we are the burning ones who live in the very presence of the burning God! This is what we are, and this is what we do.

This is the hour in which the church of Jesus Christ across the earth is recovering her identity as the great multitude.

Waiting To Get Poked

Some worshipers are like soap dispensers. I'm thinking of the kind of soap dispensers often found in public establishments, where you poke on the button and out comes a serving of hand soap. In a similar way, some worshipers act like worship dispensers. If you poke them, they'll dispense a serving of worship.

So some worship leaders have resigned themselves to the fate of continually having to poke people to get them to worship. For every time you poke them, you can figure on getting 6-10 seconds of response.

"Did you say something? I can't hear you out there!"

"Put your hands together and give it up for Jesus!"

"If you're saved and you know it, let me hear you shout!"

People have learned to respond on cue. When they're poked, they respond for a few seconds, and then it's back to the former levels of passivity. An enthusiastic worship leader can get a compliant congregation to do most anything for six seconds.

When worship leaders poke us to get us to worship, they're not challenging our manhood; nor are they challenging our womanhood. They're challenging our *multitudehood.* It's time that we awakened to who we are. "'Awake, you who sleep, arise from the dead, and Christ will give you light'" (Ephesians 5:14). We are the great multitude! We stand on the sea of glass! We have a river of fire coursing through our being. The time has come for us to stand up and be counted!

It's totally unfair for us to lay on the worship leaders the burden of getting us to worship God. It's impossible for the leaders to ignite in our hearts whatever it takes to get us to worship. They can't lift our hearts; they can't refresh our soul; they can't satisfy our thirst; they can't turn the door of our hearts; they can't warm out spirits. Their role is to provide direction for the meeting, to bring order and cohesiveness, and to provide the best opportunity possible for us to worship. But the key to worship is at the door of each one of our hearts, and the only One with the key is the One who said, "'I have the keys'" (Revelation 1:18)—that is, the originator of the river, Jesus Christ.

We don't find our inspiration to worship from the worship leaders, but from the river.

This Belongs To Us

I, too, am a member of the great multitude. I stand with you, following the leadership of the platform ministry, seeking to enter with you into heaven's best. So from one worshiper to another, let me ask you a question.

Why do we always accept it, when *they* say the song is over?

Here's how the burning ones sometimes feel: "You might be finished with the song on the platform; go ahead and ritard into the finalé, but I'm not done with my worship. You see, I've got this fiery river flowing through my spirit, and I've got a new song bursting from my heart. So go ahead and close down your old song, but I can't stop. I've got a new song in my mouth, and I've just got to let it go. I'm so in love with Jesus, my heart is overflowing with thanksgiving and praise.

"And I'm not the only one. My buddy to my left—he's on fire, too. And he's got a new song he can't hold back. And the sister on my right? Well, she's on fire, too. In fact, our whole *row* is burning before the throne right now. As is the row across the aisle from us. As is the row behind us. We're on fire out here!"

The great multitude gathers together, not to get on fire, but because they are on fire. We don't gather because we *want* to worship; we gather because we *have been* worshiping.

So the platform says, "You may be seated." And we all sit down! What's with that?

I hope you can detect my sense of humor here. Somebody may be wondering, "Bob, are you teaching rebellion?" Well, it's a *holy* insurrection. I'm not advocating rebellion to God's appointed leaders in our midst. I'm teaching rebellion to that songlist.

I'm simply challenging the profound passivity we all too often slip into, until a lot of congregations are little more than responders to all the directives coming from the platform. As long as we stay back in that paradigm, we'll pant from a distance while the fullness of the river passes us by.

I believe in following our spiritual leaders. But it's time for our leaders to throw off the yoke of expectations in which they think we want them to follow the straight lines of the service order and the songlist. We don't want the list; we want the river!

When we rise up in our identity as the multitude before the throne, and instead of waiting for the platform to poke us, we burn before God with holy passions, let me assure you of this: The leaders and worship team will not feel like we are rebelling against authority. Far from it! This is the moment they've been praying for. All their labors have been toward this one thing. When we find our place of proactive worship at the throne of God, our leaders will thrill at the mighty flow of the river with which God is graciously visiting us.

We live before the throne all week long. We gaze

upon His glory all week long. When we gather together for corporate worship, it's like heating the furnace seven times hotter. My fire joins with your fire, and the zeal we each have for the face of Christ is actually compounded and spread contagiously between all the members as we burn together in corporate worship.

When you come to the meeting on fire, you don't care what song they sing—whether it's fast or slow, high or low, new or old, loud or soft. The song doesn't dictate your worship; the internal river of fire dictates your worship. You're ablaze with holy zeal, so they could sing "Mary Had A Little Lamb" for all you care. You don't need to be poked because you're standing in the river. With the slightest opportunity, you're gone!

The Voice of the Multitude

> Then I looked, and behold, a Lamb standing on Mount Zion, and with Him one hundred and forty-four thousand, having His Father's name written on their foreheads. And I heard a voice from heaven, like the voice of many waters, and like the voice of loud thunder. And I heard the sound of harpists playing their harps (Revelation 14:1-2).

John hears a great voice from heaven, "like the voice of many waters, and like the voice of loud thunder." Whose voice is that? God's? No. God's voice does, in fact, sound like that. But in this instance, the voice John hears belongs to the one hundred and forty-four thousand. It's the voice of the great multitude! It's *our* voice!

When the multitude gazes upon the Lamb, they can't help it—their voice erupts like mighty claps of thunder.

It's time for this great multitude to find its voice. When

the church of Jesus is assembled together in His name, we are the great multitude. We have a voice like many waters and like loud thunder. This is our voice, and the time has come to exercise it.

The platform has a pretty strong voice, too. They've got microphones, speakers, instruments, drums, singers, etc. But we've got something they don't have. We have a voice like many waters and like loud peals of thunder. All we need to do is use it.

I've looked at the platform's voice (microphones, speakers, etc.), and I've looked at our voice. I've done the math. And here's my conclusion: *I think we can take them.*

"Go ahead and close down your worship if you're finished; but I'm not finished. Nor are my friends. We're the great multitude, we're on fire with God's passions, and we've got to sing our new song to the One who redeemed us by His blood." When the great multitude finds its voice, the platform doesn't stand a chance.

The Great Transition

I've been using humor to point to something, but now let me get to the bottom line. I've been trying to paint a picture for you, to give you a vision for what could be. But I want to be unmistakeably clear about where I'm going with this. *There is a transition to be found in corporate worship that is rarely discovered, but is altogether glorious once we enter into it.* Find this transition and you'll taste a little bit of heaven on earth.

Virtually all worship gatherings start off with the platform ministry serving as the initiators, and the congregation as the facilitators. This is proper and good. For a worship service to launch, it is necessary that we have appointed Levites who are prepared to initiate leadership for the worship experience. They use old songs to gather us and new songs to move us forward in the river.

Almost all gatherings of corporate worship start and end, however, with the platform serving as the initiators and the congregation as the facilitators. In most meetings, the transition never happens.

There is a transition to be found—to be strained toward, to be contended for—in which the congregation rises to its identity as the great multitude, takes ownership of the worship service, and becomes the initiators of worship. When the worship time becomes the domain of the great multitude, then the platform ministry becomes the facilitators of that which is being generated by the multitude.

When this transition happens in corporate worship, the dynamics are absolutely powerful and heavenly. We move out of the rigid preparation of our songlist into the river of God; a new song begins to arise from the hearts of God's people; the multitude finds its voice and rises up, like loud thunder, to take ownership of their place before the throne of God and to initiate their passionate praise to the Lover of their souls; the worship leaders become the facilitators of what is deriving from the multitude, supporting and helping it to maintain momentum; the glory of God fills the house of worship; we're now in swimming depth where miracles and healings are happening; a prophetic spirit falls in the place, causing the hearts of unbelievers to be laid bare, and they fall on their faces, worshiping the One who is seated on the throne.

"Oh what a foretaste of glory divine."

CHAPTER Eleven

A Lamb Fixation

Come now to the next verse in Revelation 14:

> They sang as it were a new song before the throne, before the four living creatures, and the elders; and no one could learn that song except the hundred and forty-four thousand who were redeemed from the earth (Revelation 14:3).

The saints are singing a new song before the throne, and it says that the four living creatures and the elders could not "learn" the song. This is intriguing to me. Why can't they learn the new song? Are they new song-challenged? No. Back in Revelation 5:8-9 it was the four living creatures and the elders who were singing a new song. But now they can't even learn this new song.

This seems strange to me. I think I know how to teach them the new song. We put the words on the screen; play the melody several times on the keyboard; sing it for them a couple times; then have them sing it over and over until they get it. Shouldn't be that hard to teach them the new song.

But yet the Scripture insists: They can't even learn the song.

So now I'm asking the question, "Why not?" What is it about this new song that means they can't even learn it?

I'm going to give you my best answer. There's no way to prove if I'm right, but here's my theory on it. The four living creatures and the elders can't learn the new song of Revelation 14:3 because *it's totally unrehearsed.*

Imagine this: Billions of believers gathered together around the throne, burning on the fiery sea of glass, gazing upon the face of Christ, and fashioning a new song together, extemporaneously, in the fiery passion of the moment. Imagine two billion believers crafting a new song together, simultaneously creating the same lyrics, the same melody, the same harmonies, and the same rhythms—as though they'd been practicing it for weeks.

And there's only one way to know what the next word will be, or what the next note will be: *You've got to be in the river.* Those not in the river of the redeemed just stand and watch it unfolding before them in absolute amazement. They want to join in, but they're totally incapable of singing this song. The song flows from within as the redeemed people of God stand in the midst of the Spirit's fiery river, a stream that galvanizes the Bride so that she can sing her own new song to her Beloved.

The River Flows Today

As already stated, this river is not only for the age to come. It's available to us today.

This river flowed at Christ's triumphal entry. "Then... the whole *multitude* of the disciples began to rejoice and praise God with a loud voice for all the mighty works they had seen" (Luke 19:37). Again, there was no worship leader at this event, just a groundswell of exuberant praise from the great multitude as they rose to praise our Lord according to His excellent greatness. The dark scowls of the critics couldn't staunch this flow of heaven-empowered celebration. The multitude had found the river, and an entire city was moved. Blessed are the people who know this joyful sound!

This river flowed in the Upper Room, on the Day of Pentecost (Acts 2). It swept the 120 disciples off their feet and carried them along in a fiery flow of declaring the praises of God. The mockers mocked, but they couldn't stop this river. A prophetic spirit fell upon Peter as he preached from this river, the secrets of men's hearts were revealed, and BOOM—3,000 souls were brought into the Kingdom and baptized in water!

This river is still flowing today. That's what Ezekiel saw, when he was shown the river. He saw this river flowing in this age, bringing healing to the nations, and producing a great harvest of "fish" for the glory of God. The river of fire from God's throne is still flowing today, and it's glory is available to those who will thirst and yearn for it.

The Lamb

What is it that empowers and energizes this Revelation 14 river? Look again at the passage.

> Then I looked, and behold, a Lamb standing on Mount Zion, and with Him one hundred and forty-four thousand, having His Father's name written on their foreheads. And I heard a voice from heaven, like the

voice of many waters, and like the voice of loud thunder. And I heard the sound of harpists playing their harps. They sang as it were a new song before the throne, before the four living creatures, and the elders; and no one could learn that song except the hundred and forty-four thousand who were redeemed from the earth (Revelation 14:1-3).

The river finds its fountainhead in the Lamb of God. As the redeemed gaze upon the Lamb, their love is awakened and enflamed, the river catches their hearts up, and the new song explodes from within.

It's the Lamb who gives us this river. His pierced side allows His liquid love to pour forth into our hearts. It's our affections for the Lamb of God that opens our hearts to this river. We're in love with the Lamb.

This Bride has a Lamb fixation. All she can see is the Lamb; all she can think about is the Lamb; all she wants to do is be with the Lamb. It's lovesickness in its fullness. Which is why the next verse says, "These are the ones who follow the Lamb wherever He goes" (Revelation 14:4). They're Lamb groupies. They will not—they cannot—be separated. He took the nails in His hands and feet, and now she is entirely His. Forever.

The Vision Summarized

So what is our vision for corporate worship? Here it is again, in a final summation. This is not worship as we hope it might happen; this is worship as it most definitely will happen—here on earth, in this age, before Jesus returns.

• God's people are gathered to worship our beloved

Savior and Redeemer. The worship leaders take us on a passionate search for the Ezekiel 47 river of God's glory.

- Once we hit water, the leaders are using their lists and preparation as guides, but the desire is to flex and flow with the river as the Spirit takes us on a fluid journey into the heart of God. So the rigid lines of the service order are set aside in favor of encountering God.

- As we move from ankle depth to knee depth to waist depth, something organic and alive begins to coalesce as our corporate worship takes on an identity all its own. A tapestry of worship emerges as the Bride and the Bridegroom alternate reciprocally in the dance of divine romance.

- As we gaze upon the beautiful Lamb of God, the old song unites and galvanizes the hearts of believers into a crescendo of high worship; but then a new song begins to erupt, thrusting us forward into the freshness of the deeper waters.

- A powerful transition begins to unfold. The saints of God rise up in confidence in their identity as the great multitude, and we begin to release a sound like many waters and like loud thunder, proactively taking ownership of the worship service. A corporate synergism takes over the multitude as we now become the initiators of worship, while the worship team steps back into a facilitating role.

- Now we are in waters which cannot be crossed, waters in which one must swim—it's where the trees of healing are. Now the Glory of God is manifest as healings and miracles and the raising of the dead burst forth in the midst.

- The Fourth Man shows up in the fire, burning away every hindrance that inhibits us from expressing ourselves freely in the fiery furnace of God's love.

- A spirit of prophecy is released, revealing the secrets of men's hearts. Sinners are falling on their faces, giving glory to God, and walking away testifying, "God is in the midst of those people!"

O holy Lamb of God, evermore lead us forward to these springs of living water!

Now to Him who is able to do exceedingly abundantly above all that we ask or think, according to the power that works in us, to Him be glory in the church by Christ Jesus to all generations, forever and ever. Amen

Order Form

Books by Bob Sorge

	Qty.	Price	Total
BOOKS:			
ENVY: THE ENEMY WITHIN	_____	$12.00	_____
LOYALTY: The Reach of the Noble Heart	_____	$13.00	_____
FOLLOWING THE RIVER: A Vision for Corporate Worship	_____	$ 9.00	_____
SECRETS OF THE SECRET PLACE	_____	$14.00	_____
Secrets Of The Secret Place COMPANION STUDY GUIDE	_____	$10.00	_____
GLORY: When Heaven Invades Earth	_____	$ 9.00	_____
PAIN, PERPLEXITY & PROMOTION	_____	$13.00	_____
THE FIRE OF GOD'S LOVE	_____	$12.00	_____
THE FIRE OF DELAYED ANSWERS	_____	$13.00	_____
IN HIS FACE: A Prophetic Call to Renewed Focus	_____	$12.00	_____
EXPLORING WORSHIP: A Practical Guide to Praise and Worship	_____	$15.00	_____
Exploring Worship WORKBOOK & DISCUSSION GUIDE	_____	$ 5.00	_____
DEALING WITH THE REJECTION AND PRAISE OF MAN	_____	$ 9.00	_____
UNRELENTING PRAYER	_____	$ 12.00	_____

SPECIAL PACKET

Buy one each of all Bob's books, and save 30%.

Call or visit our website for a current price.

Subtotal	_____
Shipping, Add 10% (Minimum of $3.00)	_____
Missouri Residents Add 7.725% Sales Tax	_____
Total Enclosed	_____

Domestic Orders Only/U.S. Funds

Send payment with order to: Oasis House • P.O. Box 127
Greenwood, MO 64034-0127

Name _____

Address: Street _____

City _____ State _____

Zip _____

For quantity discounts and MasterCard/VISA or international orders, call 816-623-9050 or order on our fully secure website: *www.oasishouse.net*. See our site for free sermon downloads.

Other Books by Bob Sorge

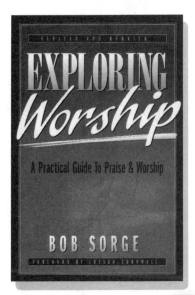

EXPLORING WORSHIP is a 300-page textbook that covers a full range of subjects related to praise and worship. Translated into several languages, this best-selling book is being used internationally as a text by many Bible colleges, Bible study groups, and worship leading teams.

This WORKBOOK/DISCUSSION GUIDE accompanies the EXPLORING WORSHIP textbook, providing a means for group interaction and the reinforcement of the book's material. Used together, these two books provide an unparalleled worship curriculum for local churches.

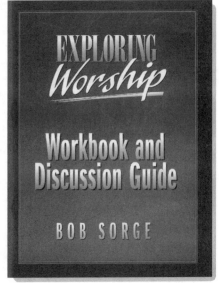

www.oasishouse.net

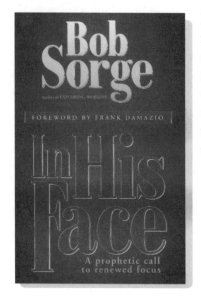

IN HIS FACE propels the reader passionately toward a more personal and intimate relationship with Jesus Christ. Intense, challenging devotional reading. This is the first book Bob wrote in the darkness.

THE FIRE OF DELAYED ANSWERS explores how God sometimes delays the answers to our prayers in order to produce godly character in us. This book is "spiritual food" for those in crisis or difficulty.

www.oasishouse.net

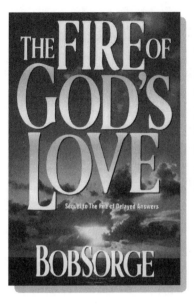

THE FIRE OF GOD'S LOVE compels us toward the passionate love that God is producing within the Bride in this hour for her Bridegroom, the Lord Jesus. Pursue the intimacy of sharing in His sufferings!

PAIN, PERPLEXITY & PROMOTION looks at the book of Job from a fresh, prophetic vantage. Job's life shows how God promotes His chosen vessels to higher heights than they would have conceived possible. You won't find a more stirring, heart-felt book on Job.

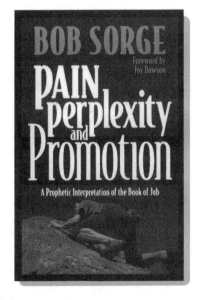

www.oasishouse.net

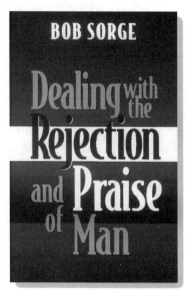

DEALING WITH THE RE-
JECTION AND PRAISE OF
MAN is a booklet that shows
how to hold your heart before
God in a way that pleases Him
in the midst of both rejection
and praise from people. Powerfully important reading for
Christian leaders.

GLORY: WHEN HEAVEN
INVADES EARTH articu-
lates the highest goal of
worship—to behold the
Glory of God. Be renewed
in the assurance that God's
Glory is coming, and let
your vision be kindled for
a personal, life-changing
encounter with God Him-
self. Especially relevant for
revivalists.

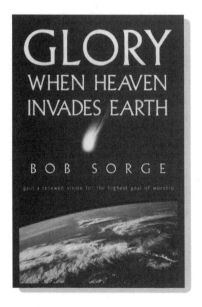

www.oasishouse.net

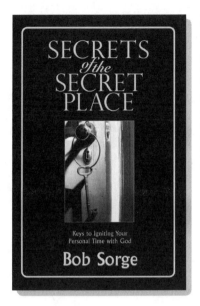

In SECRETS OF THE SECRET PLACE Bob shares some of the secrets he's learned in making the secret place energizing and delightful. This has become Bob's bestseller. Gain fresh fuel for your secret devotional life with God!

This COMPANION STUDY GUIDE, when used with the Secrets book, comprises an unparalleled curriculum for igniting believers in the exhilarating delight of sitting at Jesus' feet and hearing His word. Designed for individual and small group usage.

www.oasishouse.net

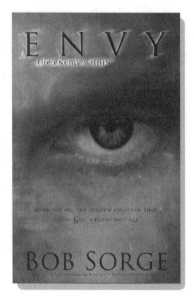

ENVY. This book reveals how ambitious motives and carnal comparisons between ministries can hinder the release of God's blessings. Explore how 2-talent saints envy 5-talent saints. Riveting and provocative.

LOYALTY: The Reach of the Noble Heart — Bob has probably put more energy into this book than any other he's written, producing what is essentially a primer on the topic of loyalty. It inspires loyalty to God and to God's Davids. The purpose of this book is to help team members understand why their leader values loyalty, and to gain a vision for the powerful potential of loyalty within a team context.

www.oasishouse.net

UNRELENTING PRAYER: Based upon the Luke 18 parable of the persistent widow, this book will increase your faith to remain fervent in prayer until God grants you justice from your adversary. Take a tender look at the issues of depression, reproach, and why God sometimes waits so long to answer our prayers. Your heart will be strengthened as you consider the restoration and restitution God intends to manifest in your life.

www.oasishouse.net